AF366713

grief and other lonely things

Laura McCann

BookLeaf
Publishing

India | USA | UK

grief and other lonely things © 2023 Laura McCann

All rights reserved.

No part of this publication may be reproduced, stored in a retrieval system, or transmitted, in any form or by any means, electronic, mechanical, photocopying, recording, or otherwise, without the prior written permission of the presenters.

Laura McCann asserts the moral right to be identified as the author of this work.

Presentation by *BookLeaf Publishing*

Web: www.bookleafpub.com

E-mail: info@bookleafpub.com

ISBN: 9789357212380

First edition 2023

For Margaret.

ACKNOWLEDGEMENT

Thanks to BookLeaf Publishing for this opportunity.

PREFACE

I've always found writing a rather cathartic hobby, and only seem to turn to it during low points in my life. I don't often reflect on my writing after it's finished, and so this whole experience was quite emotional for me. I hope you enjoy reading this as much as I enjoyed making it.

The fidelity of grief

When she meets you (and she will)
She will never leave.
She eats at my table
She sleeps in my bed
She cries in my shower again and again
and again.
Over time, you grow used to her.
Her presence is normalised and
You can almost live in peace.
Almost, but not quite.
She will fade, over time, but never
Vanish,
like a bloodstain on your life and your love,
She will remain.
Grief is the love left over for the people we have
lost.

Lena

I remember soft, grey hair
Blue eyes, pale skin, frail and thin
I remember the perfumed air
and a burgundy dress hanging from your frame.

I remember a rocking chair
A China doll, a kitchenette, a chess set
I remember the times I would stare
Down the hallway, at the door, and out you came

In fluffy red slippers and arms outstretched
as we barrelled down the hallway like
Blaring bulls, crashing into you
and holding you tight in a fierce hug.

I remember smiles and laughs, your
perfect white teeth always in sight,
I remember joy and fun and
Never sickness, only light, and

I remember the last day, like any other
My happy heart filled with love
I remember you were a little slower
The visit, a little shorter
I remember trembling hands, pressing

A beautiful snow globe into mine.
A month later, the snow globe smashed
As I sit among a sea of black
And follow your coffin to the graveyard.

My Uncle's Grave

My Uncle's grave has grown over green
long before I was born.
"Here lies David Doran,"
Gold letters on black marble
That is cold and wet with a thousand tears.

Brother, son, father, friend,
A decidedly tragic end
To a short and sorrow-filled life.

I visit, sometimes, but
Never alone
Because I feel like a liar
An imposter
As I grieve for someone I love, but had
never known.

An old milk carton, filled
with Holy Water
Sprinkled silently over that green, green grass
A quick "Hail Mary" muttered
Under breaths, as we wait
For that strained silence to pass.

I wrote letters, on occasion
Although I never left them
Because I knew he would never receive them
And I am angry
The demons I share with a man I never knew
Cry with the pain of a thousand lifetimes
As I cry to a gravestone
Instead of a man.

My Grandmother's Hands

My Grandmother's hands are firm
In their grip, although shaky
(the shakiness has become more noticeable in
recent years)
They reject help offered to them
With a defiance stronger than the branches
I swung on as a child, in happier times
When the world did not seem quite as bleak
As I now understand it to be.

Death haunted my dreams from a young age
When we buried my great grandmother
On my father's side
Never have I felt such deep loss since
(a great uncle, buried one Christmas eve – a
mystery man – an exception)
My mother's brother, dead
By his own hand, before I existed
Death has haunted me
Long before I was born.

My Grandmother's hands are finite
As all living things are finite
And it scares me, because I know
Clever girl

That Death does not haunt
Only me
He calls for all of us, and He will call for her
And she will answer
(We all answer)
And my Grandmother's hands will hold the
hands of Death
As he leads her out of our world
And into the next.

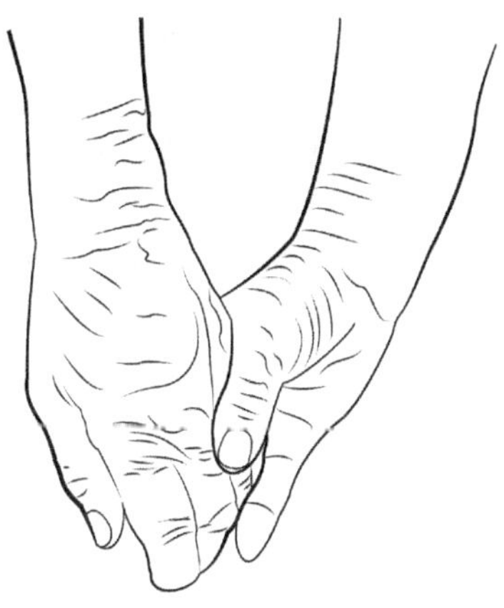

The day you left us

It's a cold February morning when
my mother wakes me, hand shaking
my shoulder, "she's gone. She's
gone." I feel nothing and everything
all at once. My heart is swelling with
pain and relief and I want to scream
and shout and never make another
noise again. What is my world
without you in it? You are no longer
in pain, but it wreaks my bones and
my soul, down to my very core.
What do I do with the love that I held
for you? Where do I put it? I can't
let it go but my arms are tired, and it is
a heavy weight to carry. I keep
thinking that you're just down the
road and it is a sobering reality
when I remember you aren't. How do
I move on? How do I live? How can I
face this again and again and
again? Twenty-one years is at once
a blessing I will cherish and
not at all enough. You are
everything. You were everything.
This pain is beating in my chest and

filling my lungs and my heart and
my throat but I can't let it out,
because what will be left when I do?
I hold this pain so I can hold what's left of you.

A love letter to an old friend

I'll watch our love die like the
flowers you never gave me and I
was too afraid to ask you for
because asking defeats the purpose
of giving flowers in the first place.

I am fascinated by our ending.
I imagined an explosion, a symphony
of screaming and crying and caring
and wanting, but we diminish like a
candle, alight one minute and
snuffed out the next. The remainder
of our love floats wispish in the air,
until the smoke is reclaimed and we
are no more.

It is not a reckoning. It
is a moment. One, singular,
miniscule moment to finalise ten
years of loving you. I think I should
feel worse than I do, but the reality
is we were over long before either of
us said anything.

I have learnt from
you and from us. I will still give my
love, but not as freely, because you
showed me that this type of love is
transactional. I give, and you take.
You give, and I give more. I will
always give more. I wanted you
because I loved you wholly. You
wanted me until I no longer needed
you. I miss you. I never want to see
you again.

To be a woman

One day, I will forgive my stomach
for her softness. I will find love for
the folds and creases, see beauty in how
she looks when I sit.

One day, I won't turn
Sideways in the mirror, to see how
My body holds herself
In a particular dress.

One day, I'll just put on the damn dress and
Fuck what other people think.
And yes,
people will stare, but
They will stare because I am strong
I am healthy
I am unashamed

This world is a cruel place
for little girls to live.
We will never be good enough for anyone else.
I want to be good enough for me.

In choosing love

I think we're expected, when we're born
To love so many people.
You're told to love
Your parents, your family, your friends.
Countless people expect you to love them.
Countless more earn that love.
But what they never tell you, when you're born,
is that
Choosing to love is
Choosing to lose and
Loving and losing is the slowest way
To kill yourself.

If love was poison

If love was poison, I think I'd drink it anyway,
Swallowing every last drop
As if I would never drink again.

If love was poison, I think I'd savour the pain
And the burning, as it made its way down
down, down
my throat and into my stomach.

If love was poison, I think I'd kill for the chance
Just to taste a drop.
I am not designed to be loved, and if
Drinking this poison meant there was a chance
That someone would love me how
I dreamed of being loved, then
Yes. I'd drink it every time.

Do not tell me that you wouldn't do the same.

You'd think you'd know when the world is falling apart

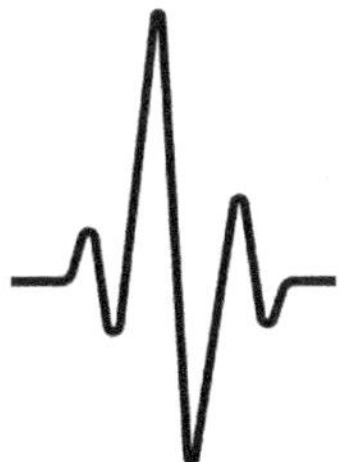

You'd think you'd know
When the world is falling apart
You'd think you'd hear
The crumbling, crashing structures
Collapsing to the ground
And the piercing screams of seven billion people

As the fragile world breaks
As easy as a twig, snapped and thrown
Onto the fire,
Lit to keep the demons away
You huddle closer, and realise
That you don't know when the world is falling
apart,
Because it starts small

A hairline fracture, embedded deep
In the essence
Of everything you hold dear
You don't realise that the flowers are dying
Until they have withered away to dust
And what was once teeming
With life, and love, and joy
Lies barren, desolate
Hostile

The hairline fracture grows, and invades
Your very being
And splits you open,
Like a coconut, cracked
Down the middle, your milk
Spilling, spoiled, over the barren world
Sour and undrinkable

And you realise, too late, that you don't know
that the world is falling apart
Until it already has.

When the Old Gods return

Zeus will not care.
Nor Hermes, nor Apollo.
Men, or men-like things
Often don't.

But Hera, protector of women,
Hera, vengeful to those who wrong
Her and her own,
Hera will care.

Artemis, the wild goddess of the hunt,
Does not just hunt animals,
No.
Artemis will care.

Athena, Persephone, Aphrodite,
Each as dangerous as they are divine,
They will care.

And when the Old Gods return,
They will not just care.
They will remember
Every hardship women have suffered under
Self-righteous men.
They will remember.
They will avenge.

They will remind the world
Why you do not fuck with women.

Aftermath

And when the dust has settled and the air
has cleared,
When I have screamed my lungs bloody and my
eyes have stopped flooding saltwater,
In the strange silence that has befallen me,
I look up and see her gentle face and ask,
"Is it over?"
She takes my hands in hers and weeps
in response, and I know
it has only begun.

YOU ARE WHAT YOU LOVE

I am tea - no sugar- with a drop of milk
and chocolate and cake and
books and poems and
crewneck sweaters,
I am hot baths and scented candles
I am music
I am orchids
I am singing, I am dancing
I am long hugs after a hard day.

I am so many different things, but
I am not myself.

An Ode to the Darkness I wear so well

I wear my Darkness like a hand-me-down coat
It was thrust upon me as a child,
And I wasn't quite sure what it meant, only
That I had to wear it

What they forgot to teach me, as a child,
Was how to remove it
And hang it
(Neatly, so as not to crease)
In the back of my wardrobe, to be taken out
As sparingly as possible, and only when my
other coats
Of happiness, love and light
Did not fit the occasion.

Forgetfulness has consequences
For when the occasion called for other coats
They never quite fit right
Over the top of my hand-me-down coat
I do not know how to take off.

Grown up now, with others around me
Offering to help me remove my coat
But I don't let them take
this hand-me-down coat because this coat,
Mistakenly worn for as long as I can remember,
Is familiar

This coat of darkness has shaped me
Moulded me
Broken me
And I can't take it off, because without it
I don't know who I am.

before derealisation

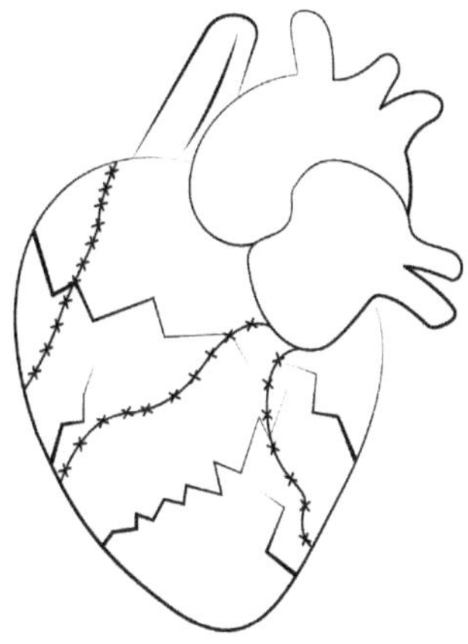

it starts in my chest and
breaks through my ribs.
it crawls up my throat until I choke and
down into my stomach.
it settles there, most times.
it waits.
and then, when I lose focus for a split second,
it's everywhere all at once.
it oozes from my skin and becomes
the air I breathe.
it leaks from my nose like a nosebleed.

I can't speak because it
weighs down my tongue.
every step I take, I drag my feet
from carrying the weight of it –
like Atlas holding the weight of the world.
it burns through my body and
turns me to ice.
it wants me to scream but it has
stolen my voice.
I am certain that, someday,
this will be what kills me.

A conversation with my therapist

"What do you think of, when you think of
yourself?"
A pause.
"I generally try not to perceive myself in that
way."
"Why?"
"It makes me uncomfortable."

"Okay. How would you describe yourself,
then?"
Another pause.
"I… don't know. Nothing positive comes to
mind."
"Can you elaborate on that?"
"Like… I can't say I'm funny, because
What if the person I say that to doesn't think I'm
funny?
And I can't say I'm kind, because
I'm not always kind, and
I can't say I'm a good person, because
How can I be the one to decide if I'm good or
not?"
"Do you think you're a good person?"
A final pause.
"… I don't think I am."

The girl I was

Green eyes hold a spark.
There's a lot she doesn't know; she can't wait
to learn. A feral, gap-toothed grin.
Eight years old and ready to rule the
world. She devours books like
a person starved, she sings loud and
laughs long. She loves fiercely and
trusts freely. There's nothing she can't do.

I stare at the photograph staring back at me.
I killed the girl I was. I grieve her every day.

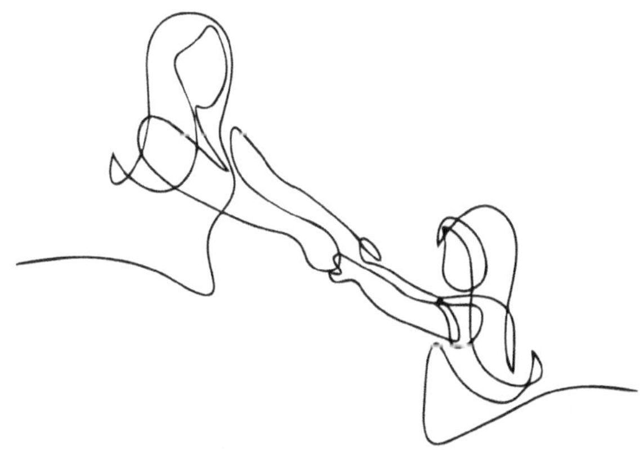

An open letter to the wide-eyed child I was before

I'm so sorry for what will happen. I wish I could prepare you; I wish I could warn you, but I can't. The world you live in is a fantasy, it isn't real. The people you idolise are not perfect, and their mistakes will hurt you in ways I cannot describe. You know who you are. That will change. There will be days when you aren't sure if you'll see the next, but I promise you, you will. Not only will you see them, but you will also find purpose, and hope, and all the other wonderful things about this life. Some days, you will crave the stability and simplicity that comes with childhood – you will mourn the loss of freedom and begrudge the shackles of adulthood and maturity. But you will live, even when you thought you wouldn't. That's what counts.